GLORY DAYS

Western Region Steam Around London

Kevin McCormack

Ian Allan PUBLISHING

CONTENTS

First published 1998

ISBN 0 7110 2611 4

Published by Ian Allan Publishing

an imprint of Ian Allan Publishing Ltd, Terminal House, Station
Approach, Shepperton, Surrey TW17 8AS.
Printed by Ian Allan Printing Ltd, Riverdene Business Park,
Molesey Road, Hersham, Surrey KT12 4RG.

Code: 9810/B3

INTRODUCTION

Glory Days: Western Region Steam Around London is a
photographic tribute to the former Great Western Railway
(GWR) in the postwar years up to the end of Western
Region (WR) steam on 31 December 1965, with a text
which combines factual information with the observations
of a schoolboy growing up in that period. I was the
schoolboy.

Before starting this work I first had to decide where
the geographic limits for the London area should be fixed.
The London Division extended from Paddington to the
Oxford area but I have drawn the line (pun intended!)
roughly 25 miles from the capital. This conveniently brings
in Maidenhead and High Wycombe as my boundaries,
which were both railway landmarks from an historical
perspective.

The title of the book gave me some difficulty. I settled
on 'Western Region Steam Around London' even though
that is somewhat inaccurate given that the Western had
just a single London terminus, with services going in only
one general direction (ie west/northwest). Admittedly, WR
locomotives could be seen elsewhere in London: on the old
West London Extension Railway at Kensington Olympia,
on empty stock workings out of Waterloo, on 'foreign'
sheds such as Willesden and Neasden when working
excursions, on the Reading–Guildford–Redhill line and,
after sale to London Transport, on the Underground.
Nevertheless, I admit that this is somewhat stretching
the term 'around London'.

As for the 'Glory Days', there was certainly a great deal of
glory around in the 1950s, particularly in the second half of
the decade, with the creation of new named express trains,
the reintroduction of the old GWR chocolate and cream
colours on express coaching stock and the adoption of
green livery with full lining-out on all classes of locomotive,
however small, that were likely to haul passenger trains.
The glory is reflected mainly in the black and white
photographs; the colour material focuses more on the final
four years, the last two of which were positively inglorious.

By then, the locomotives were generally unkempt and demoted to menial tasks. Worse still, in the final year, many were devoid of their numberplates and the 'namers' had all lost their brass nameplates. In the London area, only one resident locomotive was regularly kept clean, prairie tank No 6106; and visiting 'Castle' class loco No 7029 *Clun Castle* also retained its glory intermittently due to its frequent use on specials.

I grew up on the WR main line near Ealing Broadway. My earliest recollection of trains was peering through the wire fence at Springbridge, aged about four, and being seriously underwhelmed by the sight of the gas turbine locomotive No 18000. I think my lifelong hatred of postwar diesels and electrics started at that point! It was also about then that my father brought home for me a copy of *Trains Illustrated* (March 1951 edition) which I persuaded him to buy for me each month. I remember being petrified by a particularly gruesome photograph in the February 1952 issue depicting a Southern locomotive (No 32522) lying across a river. I quickly became expert at skipping that page!

By 1955, I had discovered Ian Allan spotting books and for the next few years spent much of my free time taking down the engine numbers, mainly at Ealing Broadway (Haven Green) or West Ealing (the milk bay or 'Jacob's Ladder'). I can remember seeing Southall's two '66xx' 0-6-2 tanks, Nos 6654 and 6655, shunting at West Ealing and the last three 'Star' class 4-6-0s speeding through Ealing Broadway (*Princess Margaret*, *Glastonbury Abbey* and *Malmesbury Abbey*). I was about 10 when I started taking photographs with my mother's prewar Box Brownie camera, one of my first shots being a close-up of the cab of push-and-pull fitted pannier tank No 5420 at Castle Bar Park Halt, with a particularly surly driver scowling at me. Luckily, this did not deter me from using the camera more and more. I was aware that British Railways' policy was wholesale dieselisation/electrification but I never imagined that the WR would be the first region to abolish steam. Although I visited the other regions, the WR was my favourite. I considered the GWR designers' locos to be aesthetically beautiful and, of course, such was the high degree of standardisation that if you liked one class, you probably liked them all. The sight of these fine engines in their last year, shuffling around in a deplorable state or lying in sidings with their motion disconnected, awaiting the call of the scrapyard, was very depressing.

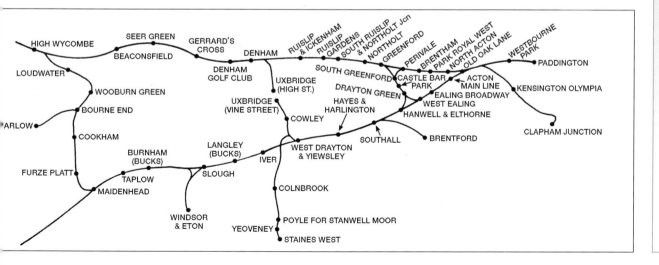

The only hope on the horizon was the fledgling private preservation movement and, in view of its London connections, the obvious Society for me to support was the Great Western Society (GWS). It was founded and had its address in Southall, its Management Council (which I later joined) met in the former stationmaster's office on Platform One at West Ealing and it had a depot at Taplow. 1965 marked the end of WR steam and there was a virtual ban on subsequent steam operation apart from some SR and LMR cross workings. Fortunately, due to its excellent relationship with WR senior management, the GWS was able to bring some cheer to the steam-starved London area. No 6106 moved from Southall depot to Taplow goods shed in spring 1966 and on 17 September 1966 no less than 7,000 visitors crammed into Taplow goods yard to have rides behind this loco and to inspect *Pendennis Castle*. The

highlight of the day was the arrival of GWS-managed 4-6-0 No 7808 *Cookham Manor* on a railtour from Birmingham, travelling via High Wycombe and the Greenford loop. Hauling a rake of LMS carriages, the loco, still in its old BR livery, produced a lovely performance which included a top speed of 79mph at Denham. After another successful Taplow open day in September 1967, when '2251' class 0-6-0 No 3205 visited from the Severn Valley Railway, the GWS set up its new permanent home at Didcot. No 6106 left Taplow for Didcot on 4 November 1967 under its own power, but this was no ordinary trip. The route was Taplow–Kensington Olympia–Taplow–Didcot–Oxford–Didcot! The diversions were made in order to collect some coaches for export which were to be temporarily stabled at Didcot. I believe that this was the last steam-hauled working of a GWR loco in the London

1962 was the last year of the 'Kings' and Old Oak Common was proud to use them on the prestigious Newbury race specials right to the end. In August 1962 No 6021 *King Richard II* is ready to leave Platform 2 at Paddington. *Geoff Rixon*

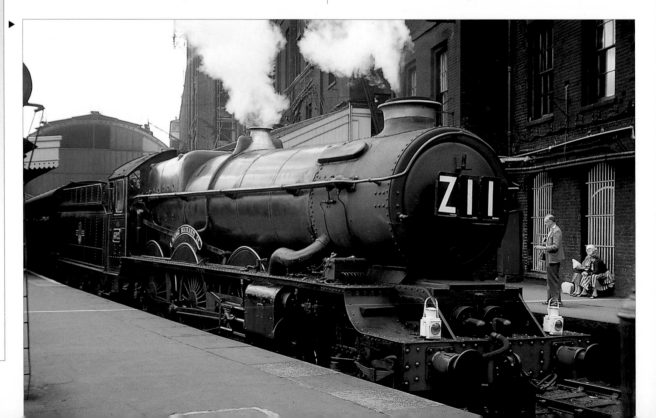

◀ Another resplendent 4-6-0, No 5014 *Goodrich Castle*, prepares to depart from Paddington in July 1962. *Geoff Rixon*

area for four years, by which time a new era for steam was dawning – but that's another story.

In compiling this book, I found it useful to have the contemporary reports which I wrote between the ages of 13 and 15 for a railway newsletter I produced for friends. Regarding the photographs, these are arranged, wherever possible, in geographical sequence (subject to the colour/black and white mix) with a batch towards the centre of the book focusing on the engine sheds in the area. As well as covering normal operations, I have also selected material featuring more unusual workings and I hope that none of the photographs has been seen before. I am very grateful to the various photographers whose material has augmented my own: Mike Esau, Roy Hobbs, Colin Hogg, Vernon Murphy, Trevor Owen, Geoff Rixon

and Tony Wright. Thanks also go to Peter Chatman, Peter Lemar and Charles Whetmath of the GWS for their help, as well as to my daughter Amber for assistance with proofreading.

Finally, a thank you to the late Dai Woodham for failing to scrap (and therefore saving) around 100 Western locos at Barry and also to all those who have enabled us to enjoy Western steam running out of Paddington again, even if we now have to go west of Hayes & Harlington to escape the new overhead electric paraphernalia for the Paddington-Heathrow rail link.

Kevin R. McCormack
Ashtead, Surrey
August 1998

1. THE MAIN LINES TO THE WEST AND NORTHWEST

When the 27-year-old Isambard Kingdom Brunel was appointed Civil Engineer to the GWR in 1833, he had a vision of being able to travel from London to New York via Bristol by steam. This book covers the main line as far as Maidenhead which was the first section of the GWR to open. On 4 June 1838, the broad gauge locomotive *North Star* hauled the inaugural train, a directors' special, from the original Paddington station, built on railway arches slightly to the northwest of the present station, to the first Maidenhead station, ¼-mile west of today's Taplow station.

As the railway grew, Brunel wanted a more fitting London terminus and, with the help of his friend Digby Wyatt, created a magnificent cathedral which was completed in 1854. Paddington station is still comparatively unchanged apart from the addition of a fourth roof span in 1913-6 and the integration of Bishop's Road underground station into the main station in 1933. Other engineering masterpieces of Brunel's are also still in everyday use: the Wharncliffe viaduct at Hanwell where Queen Victoria is said to have had the train halted to admire the splendid view over the Brent Valley (still relatively unchanged, looking north) and Maidenhead bridge across the River Thames, with the flattest brick arches in the world at the time and which Brunel's critics were convinced would collapse.

When the line was built, there were only two tracks, broad gauge of course. The addition of a second pair of tracks involved the widening of the bridges and viaducts (the original façade of the Wharncliffe viaduct is the southern side with the coat of arms) and the reconstruction of the stations. Over the years many of these have been rebuilt but Victorian survivors can be found, the most original of which is Hanwell and Elthorne, reluctantly restored by BR in 1973 as part of a deal allowing demolition of the down main line building and platform. Slough station has also survived relatively unscathed: it has retained its attractive ironwork on the

roof domes and its stuffed dog ('Station Jim') which died on 19 November 1896 and stands in a glass cabinet on the up suburban platform.

As well as serving routes to the West Country and South Wales, Paddington was also the terminus for the so-called Birmingham line to Shrewsbury and Birkenhead, but this was long after Brunel's time. In fact it was 1910 before the direct route via Bicester was opened, heralding, at least initially, the introduction of 2hr trains to Birmingham in competition with the LNWR's Euston services and knocking 20min off the fastest time via Oxford as well as shortening the distance from 129 to 110 miles.

The building of the Acton to High Wycombe section was linked with the construction of the line from West Ealing to Greenford (see page 58) and coincided with the opening of the Royal Agricultural Show by King Edward VII in 1903 at a greenfield site to be known as Park Royal. Visitors were able to travel there by a circular route to and from Paddington via North Acton, Greenford and West Ealing, and also from Southall. The show was unsuccessful and part of the site became Park Royal goods yard but the door was opened to a complex network of operations mainly involving push-and-pull services operating over both main lines. From 1910 to 1912, the GWR even tried running expresses from Birmingham to Victoria, continuing to use this London terminus until 1915 for its well-established local services from Southall. Reaching Victoria became possible through the opening, in 1863, of the joint GWR/LNWR West London Extension Railway to Kensington Olympia (formerly Addison Road) and Clapham Junction. The GWR and BR(W) continued to use the WLER for freight services and passenger excursions and in October/November 1967 several main-line services terminated at Kensington Olympia during major resignalling and engineering works at Paddington.

The auto trains from Paddington and Old Oak Lane along the Birmingham line ceased when the Central Line

Following the initial withdrawal of 27, and later all 30 'King' class locomotives in January/February 1956, the WR borrowed four mighty Stanier Pacifics from the LMR. On 16 February, No 46254 *City of Stoke-on-Trent* leaves Paddington on the 11.15am 'Merchant Venturer' to Bristol. *Colin Hogg*

No 46210 *Lady Patricia* passes North Acton on the 9am 'InterCity' from Paddington to Bristol on 16 February 1956. *Colin Hogg*

'Modified Hall' No 6977 *Grundisburgh Hall*, with correct Hawksworth high-sided tender, steams out of Paddington in June 1962. *Geoff Rixon*

The dieselisation of the Paddington-Birmingham-Birkenhead services from 10 September 1962 sounded the death knell for the remaining 'King' class locomotives. The first double-chimneyed member, No 6015 *King Richard III*, pulls into Paddington on 16 August 1962. *Geoff Rixon*

tube was extended to West Ruislip in 1948 and the old halts were quickly abandoned. I well remember, on walks with my parents from Pitshanger Lane (Brentham) to Park Royal, to see the Guinness herd of cows, going via Brentham Halt Road and asking what a 'Halt Road' meant! Steam express services continued over the line until the last 'King' class 4-6-0s were replaced by diesel hydraulics in September 1962. Then, once electrification of the Euston line was completed in March 1967, all the Birmingham line express services from Paddington were withdrawn. Local services now use Marylebone apart from one train a day in each direction (on weekday mornings), presumably for route familiarisation in the event of engineering work diversions and to avoid formal closure procedures.

Before ending this chapter, reference should be made to the joint lines in the London area in which the GWR had an interest. The WLER has already been mentioned. There was also the section of the Birmingham line from Northolt Junction to High Wycombe and beyond (to Ashendon South junction) which was jointly operated by the GWR and the Great Central Railway after the latter company had built the last new main line into London (Marylebone) in 1897. Finally, the GWR ran passenger trains along the Metropolitan Railway to Moorgate until September 1939, as well as freight workings to Smithfield Market using the 11 specially designed pannier tanks (Nos 9700-10) fitted with condensing apparatus to reduce smoke pollution on the Underground.

In 1957, the record-breaking 4-4-0 No 3440/3717 *City of Truro* was exhumed from York Museum for use on railtours. In between times, the locomotive undertook some light duties in normal service but it came as a surprise when, in the summer of 1958, it was rostered to haul fast commuter trains in and out of Paddington. Working up on the 7.30am from Reading, *City of Truro* is seen venturing to Slough and Reading on the 6.20pm, firstly at Paddington, then at Westbourne Park and, on 21 August 1958, passing through West Ealing.
Mike Esau (top right)/Colin Hogg (far right, bottom)

Empty stock workings to and from Old Oak Common carriage sidings and Paddington were usually handled by the deceptively powerful pannier tank classes ('1500', '5700' or '9400'). No 3618, a member of the 863-strong '5700' class, enters Paddington station in March 1964. *Author*

▶

Standing at Paddington's Platform 10 in August 1962 is the former No 7013 *Bristol Castle* which exchanged identity with No 4082 *Windsor Castle* in 1952 in order to haul King George VI's funeral train to Windsor because the original engine was under repair. The exchange was never reversed. *Geoff Rixon*

▶▶

Spare a thought for the residents living above the smoky hole at Ranelagh Bridge, which was the servicing yard ¼-mile outside Paddington for express engines not returning to Old Oak Common. This early postwar view shows No 5030 *Shirburn Castle* in GWR livery. *Eric Treacy*

This unfamiliar view of Paddington station depicts push-and-pull pannier tank No 5420 standing on the electrified Metropolitan Line track at Platform 15 while working the 2.55pm to Greenford on 4 July 1954. *Colin Hogg*

Prairie tank No 6149 heads a down local through Westbourne Park in 1958. The 70 members of this class, built between 1931 and 1935, were virtually exclusive to the London area for most of their lives, having a higher boiler pressure than similar classes to improve acceleration between the numerous stops. *Mike Esau*

'Castle' class No 5057 *Earl Waldegrave* receives some admiring glances as it stands beneath Bishop's Bridge at the end of Paddington's Platform 1 in June 1962. *Geoff Rixon*

The 'Castle' locomotive with the largest nameplate, No 5017 *The Gloucestershire Regiment, 28th 61st* (formerly *St Donats Castle*) backs out of Paddington after bringing in an express. *Geoff Rixon*

2. THE FINAL FLING OF THE 'CASTLES'

The early 1960s witnessed the continuing decline in the number of steam-hauled express trains out of Paddington, a trend which became all too evident in the autumn of 1962 with the withdrawal of the last of the GWR's (and for many years Britain's) most powerful locomotives, the 'Kings'. But whereas only 30 'Kings' had been constructed, the slightly less powerful but more versatile 'Castle' class had been built in much larger numbers over a very long time-span (1923 to 1950) and many were still at work when the 'Kings' were finally replaced by diesels.

There had originally been 171 'Castles' built although they were not all in service together due to the withdrawal of the first member, No 100 *A1 Lloyds* (formerly No 4009 *Shooting Star*) in March 1950, just before the last members of the class entered service. In fact, the actual number of new 'Castles' built was 156, the balance being made up of 14 converted 'Stars' and the unique GWR Pacific, No 111. Like the mighty 'Kings', the 'Castles' were capable of running at very high speeds of 100mph or more and in the 1930s Old Oak Common used to provide a 'Castle' for what was billed as the world's fastest train, the 'Cheltenham Flyer'. The service was scheduled to travel the 77.3 miles from Paddington to Swindon in 65min at an average speed of 71.4mph. On 5 June 1932, No 5006 *Tregenna Castle*, completed the journey in an incredible 56min 47sec.

At the beginning of 1964 it occurred to Ian Allan Limited that the 60th Anniversary of *City of Truro's* record-breaking run on the Plymouth to Paddington Ocean Mails Express was approaching, when a speed in excess of 100mph was recorded. What better way to celebrate this historic event than to run a railtour over the same line and achieve 100mph for almost certainly the last time with a steam locomotive and, unlike *City of Truro's* train, carry fare-paying passengers? With no 'Kings' left in service, only 'Castles' were capable of reaching this speed, but the ranks of this fine class were rapidly dwindling. Nevertheless, the Western Region was very enthusiastic

and set about planning the great day which was to be 9 May 1964 – the actual anniversary date.

It was decided that the journey would be split into three legs using different locomotives. The train would consist of seven coaches and each engine would have two firemen on board. The Chief Mechanical Engineer's department would identify eight 'Castles' with mileages below 40,000 since last overhaul. A Running Inspector would then ride on the locomotives and select the best three, with the remainder kept as reserves. Since all the engines had run over 30,000 miles, the valves, pistons and valve gears needed to be removed for examination and rectified where necessary. This work, which was carried out at Worcester and Swindon running sheds, caused the deselection of some of the more favoured engines as a result of unforeseen damage being discovered and enabled the oldest operational 'Castle', No 4079 *Pendennis Castle*, which had initially been passed over due to its age and early design, to enter the running. This was the 'little' engine which had embarrassed the LNER when it outperformed its mighty Gresley Pacific during the interchange trials of 1925.

After examination, the eight selected engines were each tried on the 9.15am ex-Paddington and 1.15pm ex-Worcester between 24 March and 27 April 1964, these services being among the few still regularly steam hauled. During the tests it became clear that in order to achieve the desired 25% cut off with full regulator opening, all eight locomotives would have to return to Swindon for repairs to their injectors and be subsequently retested in service. By now, time was running short.

At last, the Running Inspector, having ridden on all the locomotives at least once, was able to rate them according to performance. The best one was deemed to be No 5054 *Earl of Ducie* followed by, in descending order of perceived ability, Nos 4079 *Pendennis Castle*, 7029 *Clun Castle*, 7023 *Penrice Castle*, 7008 *Swansea Castle*, 7032 *Denbigh Castle*,

7022 *Hereford Castle* and 7025 *Sudeley Castle*. It is interesting that the best two were in fact the oldest, dating from 1923 and 1936 respectively, whereas No 7029 was built in 1949. However, the expert view was that providing decent coal was obtained, there was little to choose in performance between the original design of 'Castle' and the final development with high superheating and double chimney. The final allocation was Paddington–Plymouth (No 4079), Plymouth–Bristol (No 7029) and Bristol–Paddington (No 5054).

The event captured the imagination of railwaymen and enthusiasts alike because of the unlikelihood of the run ever being repeated and the desire for the 'Castles' to go out in a blaze of glory. 9 May dawned a beautiful sunny day and 40-year-old *Pendennis Castle* looked magnificent. I photographed the train going through Ealing on its outward journey (see page 20) and then went to Paddington in the evening to see *Earl of Ducie* pull in (see page 21). Excitedly, I asked people around me which engines had reached 100mph and could hardly believe the response. No 4079 had broken down while travelling at 96mph, No 7029 had managed just 97mph but No 5054, on which so many hopes had been pinned, had reached only 94mph. The magic 'ton' had not been achieved. So after all the painstaking efforts that had been made to ensure success, what went wrong?

In fact, the venture was not a failure but it was dogged by bad luck. No 4079 was running almost 6min early when the Mechanical Inspector on the train spotted burning cinders falling on the track and pulled the communication cord. But for his alertness, 100mph might have been reached, although the hot coals were already damaging the axleboxes. Of course, no one could have foreseen that the firebars would be defective. Yet very little time was lost. A totally unprepared 'Modified Hall', No 6999 *Capel Dewi Hall*, arrived within minutes from Westbury and put up a very spirited performance, achieving a speed of 86mph, before being substituted by the relief 'Castle', No 7025, at Taunton.

The next leg from Plymouth to Bristol, handled by *Clun Castle*, was spectacular despite the locomotive attaining only 97mph (at Norton Fitzwarren). At the top of Whiteball summit, No 7029 was travelling at 67mph compared with *City of Truro's* 52mph, indicating that the 'Castle' should have been easily capable of exceeding the *City's* 100mph speed on the descent. As it was, 94mph was reached before the 80mph speed restriction at Wellington put paid to achieving a 'ton'. Ironically, track works had been carried out so that the limit could be raised for this run but apparently the footplate crew had not been informed! No 7029 then proceeded to travel the 25.2 miles from Bridgwater to Nailsea & Backwell in 17min 15sec at an average speed of 87.6mph. This was the fastest time ever recorded between Exeter and Bristol and the train arrived nearly 10min early. By all accounts, the locomotive was never seriously put under pressure and on no part of the journey was the regulator more than three-quarters open.

Finally, it was the turn of No 5054, on which some unfair criticism was heaped at the time. No one can say for certain why the locomotive failed to reach 100mph on the 1 in 300 falling gradient to Little Somerford: high winds, too many open carriage windows, the wrong valve cut off and regulator opening have all been suggested. But the engine still performed admirably. Besides achieving 94mph (96mph in some reports), 5054, hauling an extra 5 tons, came within 1¾min of beating the record of 93min 50sec set by No 7018 *Dryslwyn Castle* for the journey from Bristol to Paddington on 28 April 1958. As it was, *Earl of Ducie* ran start-to-stop at an average speed of 74mph, passing Old Oak Common, only three miles outside Paddington, while still doing 82mph and reaching the terminus 4½min early. The 74½ miles from Swindon to Old Oak was actually covered in 53min 2sec, giving an average speed of 87.6mph.

It is clear therefore that 5054 was no poor performer. On the contrary, the locomotive had attained 102mph at Honeybourne on the eight-coach 3.15pm from Paddington to Worcester on 1 April 1964 while under test. And just to show that it was suffering no ill effects from the 9 May trip, 5054 clocked 95mph at Honeybourne a week later while performing a 320-mile round trip from Paddington

The 40-year-old locomotive that so nearly achieved 100mph until disaster struck: No 4079 *Pendennis Castle* passes under Spring Bridge, Ealing, on 9 May 1964, on the first leg of the 60th Anniversary special commemorating *City of Truro's* record-breaking run. *Author*

for the Oxford University Railway Society. It was tragic, therefore, that this fine locomotive should be ignominiously cut up in 'C' shop at Swindon Works in November 1964.

Luckily, the other two principal performers fared better. *Pendennis Castle*, although withdrawn on the spot, was purchased for preservation almost immediately by Mike Higson and after various changes of ownership is now in Australia.

Clun Castle went on to become the last of its class in service and, although withdrawn on 31 December 1965 along with the rest of WR steam, appeared on freight trains in the Midlands during 1966 following purchase for the Birmingham Railway Museum at Tyseley.

The 60th Anniversary run did not achieve everything that it was meant to but it was still a triumph in terms of the performances of locomotives in the twilight of their working lives and a fitting testimonial to the remarkable 'Castle' class. From then on it was all downhill: the WR's pride in its steam fleet disappeared and the remaining 'Castles', indeed the entire stock of steam locomotives, quickly deteriorated both mechanically and cosmetically.

◀ No 5054 *Earl of Ducie* on arrival at Paddington after an exceptionally fast run on the final leg of the 60th Anniversary special on 9 May 1964. *Author*

3. PRESERVATION OF THE PIONEER 'CASTLE'

When C. B. Collett produced the first of his 'improved Stars', No 4073 *Caerphilly Castle* in 1923, he launched a class which would haul express trains for 40 years and be built over a period of 27 years. Furthermore, the 'Castles' were to have a major influence on other railway companies: the LNER modified its Gresley Pacifics following *Pendennis Castle's* success in the 1925 interchange trials; and the LMS apparently considered ordering 'Castles' after borrowing No 5000 *Launceston Castle* in August 1926 but decided instead to build the 'Royal Scot' class. No 5006 *Tregenna Castle* set a speed record working the 'Cheltenham Flyer' and the class also received royal patronage when HM King George V drove No 4082 *Windsor Castle* and HM The Queen (when she was still Princess Elizabeth) named the last member, No 7037 *Swindon*, in 1950.

It was hardly surprising, therefore, that when BR announced its limited selection of locomotives to be preserved, No 4073 was on the list. The engine was withdrawn from Cardiff Canton shed in May 1960 and presented to the Science Museum in London where it arrived on 4 June 1961. It seemed that it would be incarcerated there for ever, isolated from other GWR locos. What a joy, therefore, when, 35 years later, *Caerphilly Castle* was back on rails again, standing beside fellow 'Castle', No 5051 *Earl Bathurst*, on 25 September 1996 at Didcot Railway Centre where it will remain until its new home is ready at Swindon! My contemporary account of what we all thought was No 4073's last journey in 1961 now follows:

On Friday 2 June 1961, *Caerphilly Castle* was handed over to the Science Museum in a ceremony at Paddington Station. The next day it was at Park Royal Goods Yard, coupled up to No D4004. I paid it a visit (with Nigel Collins) at 10.30am and found the tender was separated from the engine and about to be loaded on a Pickford's trailer. The engine was absolutely dazzling in the

sunlight, even the inside of the frames had been painted (orange). All the dials and cab controls were shining and the coupling rods too. The lining was in the original GWR colour, a thick black line with two narrow orange lines. On the front bufferbeam was a transfer '4073' and the buffers were covered with sacking so that they would not be marked by the diesel. The tender was an original one, a low one like those now fitted to 'Manors', and it had 'Great Western' with the coat of arms on the tender sides. I took four pictures of the engine and tender immediately. We returned to Park Royal at 11.15am and the tender was loaded on the trailer. The track had been raised up on to the trailer. I returned yet again, this time with Scott, at 7.30pm to see that the engine had been loaded on to a very long trailer and was parked near the gate, ready to leave at 8am next morning, Sunday, for the Science Museum. Scott and I agreed to come at 7.30am on Sunday, in case it left early, to avoid traffic. When we arrived we found quite a few people already there, most of whom had cameras. At about 7.45am three Pickford towing tractors arrived, followed by three policemen on motorbikes, followed by a police sergeant in an Austin Cambridge. Pat Whitehouse, secretary of the Tallylyn Railway and John Adams, both from 'Railway Roundabout' arrived in a Morris Minor, with all their cameras. John Adams was later seen on top of a brick wall with a cine-camera! It was not till 8.25am that the procession began to move. One of the towing tractors left the yard and went round a corner and the three policemen on motorbikes left the gate. Then the trailer with the engine began to move. It took three attempts to get round into the road, and when at last it did, another towing tractor with the tender followed. By going round the right of a 'keep left' sign, the engine got round the corner and stopped in the middle of the road. The other towing tractor backed on the front of the first one, making a double-header! Then the procession continued,

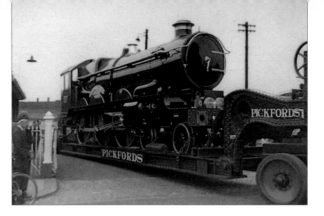

right up the middle of the road: two twin tractors, and the trailer with the engine, then another towing tractor hauling a trailer with the tender, then a little tractor with a little trailer with large blocks of wood on, and then a long line of cars and buses, and the crane following up at the rear. By going the wrong way along a 'one way' road into Horn Lane, the procession reached Western Avenue and then, going at about 10mph, the tractors, trailers and engine set off on their laborious trek to Kensington. They would not be able to go round any sharp corners or under any low bridges. All this time I was taking another five pictures, which was nothing compared to the number of pictures some people took! Anyway, off down Western Avenue went 4073, on its last journey, and Scott and I cycled back home, as it was 9am by this time.

◀◀ Rising like a phoenix from the ashes of 15 months before, No 4079 *Pendennis Castle*, restored to GWR livery, approaches Old Oak Common on 8 August 1965. This Ian Allan railtour to Swindon via Oxford and Worcester was the locomotive's first run in private ownership and a very creditable top speed of 90 mph was attained. *Author's Collection*

◀ Another railtour is featured here, this time on the Birmingham line. Emerging from White House Farm tunnel between High Wycombe and Beaconsfield, prior to the descent to Denham where 79mph was achieved, is No 7808 *Cookham Manor*. This Great Western Society special was heading for Taplow Open Day on 17 September 1966. *Charles Whetmath*

4. LOCOMOTIVE DEPOTS

Brunel's railway naturally needed engine sheds. Westbourne Park, which opened in 1852, releasing land occupied by the original wooden shed at Bishop's Bridge required for the approach to the new Paddington station, was in turn replaced by what the GWR somewhat optimistically described as the largest shed of its type in the world, Old Oak Common. Opening on 17 March 1906 and consisting of four roundhouses under one roof, this smoky cavern generated tremendous excitement for young locomotive spotters like myself, creeping in past the canteen or crawling through the famous hole in the fence on the nearby canal towpath. Alas, for me the halcyon days were short-lived; the roundhouses soon became emptier and the pride of Old Oak – the magnificent 'Kings' and '47xx' 2-8-0s – lay outside waiting to be towed away for scrap. Demolition of the main building began in March 1964 and the shed was closed to steam on 22 March 1965. The old 'factory' (repair shop) was converted into a diesel depot and one of the roundhouse turntables, now in the open, retained.

Southall shed was my second home, not least because it was easy to enter (and escape from!) if you used the footpath behind the AEC factory, past the little works diesel shunter and the field containing Ted Brewer's donkeys. I was convinced that the shed foreman never ventured out to the back of the shed yard. Not for me the bravery (or folly) of descending the steps of the footbridge at the front of the shed.

The Southall that I knew, and which happily still exists today as home to various preserved locomotives, was an eight-road through shed, built in 1953-4 to replace the previous six-road dead-end building dating from 1884. Less glamorous than Old Oak because of its allocations of mixed traffic locomotives, it nevertheless provided variety right through to the end of WR steam on 31 December 1965, having absorbed the residual steam allocations of Old Oak and Slough sheds. Southall lost its steam

allocation on 14 September 1965 although it remained a stabling point for steam. In the final months there seemed to be a proliferation of LMS locos, mainly 'Black Fives' or 2-8-0s, but occasionally a 'Jubilee' or 'Britannia'. Engines on their way to the scrapyards also lingered there for a while, including, for some strange reason, a batch of LMS 'Jinty' 0-6-0 tanks. Pride of place at Southall was occupied by its resident privately preserved inmate, No 4079 *Pendennis Castle*, whose sparkling GWR livery contrasted with the grime of all the other incumbents, apart from prairie tank No 6106.

The smallest of the three mainline sheds between Paddington and Maidenhead was Slough. Located by the Windsor branch junction, this ramshackle structure dating from the late 1860s contained only tank engines: '61xx' 2-6-2s, pannier tanks and the 'Fourteeners' for the Marlow branch. The shed closed on 1 June 1964 and the buildings were demolished.

In addition to these depots, there were tiny sub-sheds for the branch locomotives at Staines, Uxbridge and Marlow, which have long since vanished.

This August 1960 view inside the WR's largest engine shed, the quadruple roundhouse at Old Oak Common, features *King Edward VIII, Oldlands Hall* and, with its distinctive straight splashers and nameplate, *County of Brecknock. Tony Wright*

◄ The last operational 'Star' class 4-6-0, No 4056 *Princess Margaret*, dating from 1914, simmers inside Old Oak Common shed on 13 May 1956. The locomotive was withdrawn in October 1957. *Tony Wright*

◄◄ The front of Southall shed featuring No 6967 *Willesley Hall* and pannier tank No 3622. *Author*

◄ At the back, Southall's last 0-4-2 tank, No 1474, is dwarfed by two ex-War Department Austerity 2-8-0s. *Author*

◀◀ Sadly, none of the 80 'Grange' class locomotives survives today. This one, No 6824 *Ashley Grange*, stands sandwiched between pannier tanks at Old Oak Common in November 1963. *Geoff Rixon*

◀ In this scene on 26 October 1963, No 7032 *Denbigh Castle* stands at Old Oak Common alongside a Hawksworth pannier tank taking on water. *Author's Collection*

5. THE 'DUKEDOGS' WESTERN REGION FAREWELL

When I was 13 I persuaded my mother to take me on my first railway holiday. I chose Towyn on the Cambrian Coast in Wales because it was the terminus of the Talyllyn Railway and in order to see the last two survivors of the 'Dukedog' or 'Earl class' 4-4-0s, Nos 9014 and 9017. The 29 members of the class were built between 1936 and 1939 to replace the late-Victorian 'Duke of Cornwall' 4-4-0s used on weight-restricted lines such as the Cambrian. By marrying 'Duke' boilers with slightly newer frames from the heavier 'Bulldog' class, the rebuilds gained a life extension while remaining within the weight limits. Names of earls were fitted or allocated to the first 20 locomotives but apparently their lordships objected because of the archaic appearance of the engines. The nameplates were therefore transferred to new 'Castle' 4-6-0s, having to be mounted on non-symmetrical backing plates because of the difference in wheel diameter.

On our arrival at Towyn on 20 July 1960, I was instantly rewarded by the sight of No 9017 hurrying past with an engineer's carriage. This was the first and last time I saw a 'Dukedog' in action on BR until, following a successful preservation appeal, No 9017 travelled to Old Oak Common on 14 February 1962 on its way to the Bluebell Railway. It has remained there ever since, except for a four-year stay at the Didcot Railway Centre from 1985 to 1989 when, for a brief period, it worked alongside the only other GWR outside-framed survivor, *City of Truro*.

'Dukedogs' visited London only rarely and my account of the last occasion follows:

On 3 February 1962, I received an unexpected letter from Mr T. R. Gomm, telling me about the 'Dukedog' No 9017 to whose preservation I had subscribed the princely sum of 15s. The fund had reached £1,500 and the engine was ready to be purchased. It had been in store since November 1960 at Oswestry Works.

The engine ran light from Oswestry to Brighton via Old Oak Common on 14 and 15 February, leaving Oswestry at 7am and arriving at Old Oak Common at 2.26pm, where it stayed overnight. I obtained permission to be excused games at school and set off at 1.30pm to cycle to North Acton LTE station while my companions, Chris Scott and John Churchman, went to Hanger Lane. When I arrived at North Acton I locked up my bicycle and walked down the railwayman's entrance, and across a little bridge over the Central Line. Then I found there was a high fence between me and the main line, where it joins the Bristol and the West line, at Old Oak Common junction. I was forced to climb over the fence by the small bridge and walked a few yards to a suitable spot by the line. I still had 15min to wait, and two 'Kings' went by, the second one being No 6001, and No 5017 descended on a parcels train to run by the Central Line to White City, and thence to Kensington. The 'Dukedog' appeared dead on time, and fortunately the signal a few yards away from me was at danger. The 'Dukedog' whistled furiously and stopped. I ran along the side of the track and took photos of it at the signal, before running back to my previous position, so that when the signal was down, I took a photo of it coming past me. As it disappeared round the curve to join the other line, I climbed back over the fence and made my way to the shed. I had no shed-pass but I hoped to wangle my way round.

When I at length arrived at the entrance, I nipped past the canteen and down a little path which leads to the back of the shed. I arrived there and entered the gloomy shed. The place was full of engines but I was not able to see the 'Dukedog'. I asked a railwayman if he knew where it was, and having asked whether the 'Dukedog' was a diesel, was told it would be outside. And there I found it, under the coaling stage, and when I arrived there were two other photographers, and the fireman was clearing out the clinker. The Foreman rolled along to see what was what but fortunately took no notice of me. The engine then took on coal, and after half an hour went into the shed. By now it was after 3 o'clock and as nobody seemed to mind my presence, I wandered round the shed. I found No 6000 being painted and cleaned to pull the Queen Mother to Newbury Races the following day. The buffer-beam and buffers were wet with paint

and cleaners were polishing up the rest of the paintwork. The inscription on the bell was becoming indecipherable because the brass was worn, too much cleaning no doubt! At 4.40pm I left the shed and made my way back to my bicycle at North Acton station.

And so a most interesting afternoon ended, no doubt marking the last time a GW 4-4-0 would visit Old Oak.

These scenes depict the sole surviving 'Dukedog', No 9017, on its final BR journey from Oswestry to the Bluebell Railway in Sussex on 14 February 1962. The first photograph was taken between North Acton and Old Oak Common, and the remainder when the engine arrived on shed before entering the roundhouse for its overnight stay. *Author*

The arrival at Southall of six redundant light prairie tanks from the West Country in 1964 was a big surprise since these engines were virtually unknown in the London area in the postwar years. The driver of No 5545 finds time to chat during shunting operations at the shed. *Author*

The '2800' class was introduced in 1903, being the first 2-8-0s in Britain. No 2859 was the last locomotive to be repaired at Stafford Road, Wolverhampton, and left the works for its home shed of Pontypool Road on 11 February 1964. Nearly a year later, the loco is seen at Southall having arrived, judging by the tarpaulin, on a wet day. No 2859 now resides at the Llangollen Railway. *Author*

Thirteen of the old-style low-cabbed pannier tanks had an extended lease of life through being purchased by London Transport to replace its elderly steam fleet on freight workings. This view of No L89 (formerly No 5775) and L94 (formerly No 7752) at LT's Neasden shed was taken during a GWS visit in November 1969 to inspect withdrawn locomotives for potential purchase. Both these locomotives survive, on the Keighley & Worth Valley Railway and at the Birmingham Railway Museum, respectively. *Author*

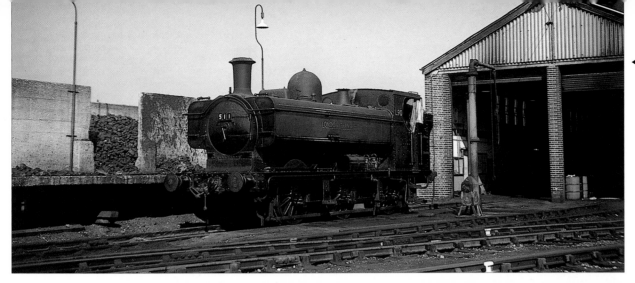

A lesser known home for LT pannier tanks was Lillie Bridge, near Earls Court, where I gained access through the good offices of an LT bus driver who had driven me (and 39 other people) to France on RTL 1050. The second No L90 (formerly No 7760), now at the Birmingham Railway Museum, stands outside the small shed in May 1969. *Author*

WR locos used to appear at the former Great Central depot at Neasden when hauling football specials to Wembley Stadium. Magnificent No 4970 *Sketty Hall* has come up from Exeter for the Schoolboys' International on 28 April 1962. *Geoff Rixon*

No 6990 *Witherslack Hall* is one of many locomotives featured in this book which escaped the scrap merchant's cutting torch. Photographed at Old Oak Common on 19 October 1963, the engine is now on the Great Central Railway. *Geoff Rixon*

Slough was the least exciting of the London sheds except when it was servicing visiting tender engines, often from other regions, which had hauled excursions to nearby Windsor. Pannier tanks Nos 3608 and 9722 represent the typical scene. *Trevor Owen*

In the final years, the sidings at the rear of Southall shed were packed with locos awaiting their final journey to the scrapyards. This collection of vintage Churchward Moguls and 2-8-0s, which includes No 5380 with buckled running plate and No 2841, was photographed in April 1964. No 5380 had a brief moment of glory on 9 June 1960 when it hauled the up 'Bristolian' following a diesel failure. *Author*

Southall's only clean locomotive in the final months was No 6106 but I must admit that I never followed the locomotive for a photograph: it seemed to follow me! In this view taken in the summer of 1965 at the front of Southall shed, the crew of No 6106 are satisfying the engine's thirst. *Author*

An unusual visitor to Southall in July 1965 was No L94 on its way to Eastleigh Works for overhaul. Evidence that this locomotive (formerly No 7752) was built by the North British Locomotive Co, Glasgow, rather than at Swindon can be seen from the diamond-shaped works plate. The reduced height of L94's cab compared with the later pannier tanks such as No 9495 on the left was the reason for LT choosing the earlier type, removing the cab roof overhang in order to operate within the limited clearances of the Underground tunnels. *Author*

Now one of No 6106's stablemates at Didcot, No 6998 *Burton Agnes Hall*, specially cleaned (along with No 6959 *Peatling Hall*) presumably for a railtour or similar working, generates some unpleasant smoke at Southall shed. *Author*

Storm clouds gather over Southall shed in September 1965 as resident celebrity, privately-owned *Pendennis Castle*, takes on coal. Collett 2-8-0 No 3836 simmers on one of the shed roads. *Vernon Murphy*

Churchward's final design for the GWR was the '4700' class built between 1919 and 1923. Apart from the Pacific, No 111 *The Great Bear*, these were also his largest locomotives. Most of the class of nine were based at Old Oak Common and in April 1964, just before the last survivors were withdrawn, No 4703 is pictured entering the roundhouse. *Author*

Small prairie No 5531 arrived at Southall in December 1963 looking very smart and it was sad to watch it deteriorate over the ensuing months. In April 1965, the loco had been made ready for its final journey; No 6106 made an unexpected appearance on the main line as I pressed the shutter. *Author*

In the late 1950s/early 1960s, 'Manor' class 4-6-0s were comparatively rare through Ealing and I can only recall No 7814 *Fringford Manor*, which was a Reading engine. They became more common towards the end of steam and No 7811 *Dunley Manor*, seen here at Southall in March 1965, gives just a hint of the splendour hidden beneath the grime. *Author*

This April 1965 view of the back of Southall shed features No 6952 *Kimberley Hall* in the company of a 'Tanner Oner' and an LMS 2-8-0. *Author* ▼

It was a surprise to find No 4079 *Pendennis Castle* receiving attention in Old Oak Common in early April 1964 because at that time I was not aware of the 9 May trip and thought that all the early 'Castles' such as this one were no longer in service. *Author* ▶

Crowds of people came to Southall to see No 6018 *King Henry VI* haul the 'King' farewell special on 28 April 1963. This engine had taken part in the 1948 loco exchanges (but did not excel due to poor coal) and also hauled the 50th Anniversary 'Cornish Riviera Express' on 1 July 1954 (a train which at one time was famous for having the world's longest regular nonstop run: London to Plymouth). On its final passenger journey, which started from Birmingham, No 6018 achieved 91mph at Denham hauling 440 tons (650 passengers) and having stopped for water at High Wycombe, 12 miles earlier – not a bad performance for a locomotive which had been withdrawn four months previously! *Geoff Rixon*

Three variations of pannier tank are seen here at Old Oak Common. In the foreground stands one of the 11 locomotives of the '5700' class which were fitted with condensing apparatus for working over the Metropolitan Line to Smithfield meat market. *Geoff Rixon*

WR locos seldom ran in service without their brass safety valve covers but Reading's 'Modified Hall' No 7919 *Runter Hall* is one such exception in this April 1964 view at Old Oak Common. The locos in the background include No 4701 (awaiting scrapping) and No 7032. *Author*

This grimy 'Grange', No 6829 *Burmington Grange*, appears to have taken the wrong line and ended up at Willesden on the LMR, although it is only about ½-mile away by road from Old Oak Common shed. *Author*

No 6938 *Corndean Hall*, although withdrawn in March 1965, was retained at Southall for static exhibition at Kensington Olympia in June 1965. This International Plastics 'express' also consisted of a special saloon, two Ocean saloons and a cinema coach. After its short reprieve, the loco was taken to R. S. Hayes Ltd at Bridgend for scrapping. *Author*

There is a smile for the camera from a footplateman in suit and tie as prairie tank No 6165 takes the crossover underneath the footbridge at Southall in order to enter the shed on 12 April 1959. The loco seems to be in need of a new chimney. *Geoff Rixon*

◄ In the early 1960s, the SR used some pannier tanks on empty stock workings between Waterloo and Clapham Junction carriage sidings. Nos 4672 and 4698 stand in at Nine Elms shed. *Tony Wright*

◄ The 6.28pm to Greenford enters Ealing Broadway on 15 May 1955 behind push-and-pull pannier tank No 5410. *Colin Hogg*

▲ One of Hawksworth's powerful outside-cylindered '1500' class, No 1503, is flanked by two more conventional pannier tanks, Nos 9498 and 9700, at Old Oak Common. *Author*

By late 1963, the only steam-hauled expresses into Paddington were from Hereford and Worcester. This autumnal view shows an up train hauled by No 7006 *Lydford Castle* between Longfield Avenue and Springbridge Road, Ealing. *Author*

Conveniently stopping at signals on the down main at Longfield Avenue and presumably reversing back to Southall shed is No 7029 *Clun Castle*, seen in early May 1965. Whatever I was doing here, I was certainly not expecting this working. *Author*

Old Oak Common Castle No 7024 *Powis Castle* speeds towards Ealing Broadway on a down express on 21 March 1953. *Geoff Rixon*

A 1953 view of Ealing Broadway station, 12 years before it was redeveloped and topped by an office block. 'Modified Hall' No 6976 *Graythwaite Hall* heads an up express to Paddington. Clearly the WR had no intention of allowing its painters to touch the LT Central Line part of the station. *Geoff Rixon*

Collett 2-8-0 No 3822 trundles through Ealing Broadway in 1961. This lucky escapee from Barry scrapyard is preserved at Didcot. *Author*

Although the nine large '4700' class 2-8-0s were mainly nocturnal and employed on fast freights, they were used on passenger turns in the summer. Their most prestigious turn was hauling the 'Royal Duchy' in 1958. Here, on 18 July 1959, No 4704 heads the 1.25pm Paddington-Paignton through West Ealing. *Colin Hogg*

Large prairie No 6114 hauls the 1.20pm Uxbridge (Vine Street) to Paddington past the milk depot at West Ealing on 24 January 1959. *Colin Hogg*

Small prairie No 5508 works a goods train over the Uxbridge to West Drayton branch near Cowley on 10 July 1964, immediately prior to closure of the line. *Roy Hobbs*

An unidentified 'Castle' approaches 'Jacob's Ladder', West Ealing, with a down express to Worcester and Hereford in early 1964. *Author*

No 5978 *Bodinnick Hall* draws a freight train out of the loop onto the up local line and under 'Jacob's Ladder' in summer 1962. *Author*

6. THE GREENFORD BRANCH

The GWR Act of 1897 authorised the Acton to High Wycombe, and West Ealing (then called Castle Hill) to Greenford lines and the latter opened on 15 June 1903, in time for the Royal Agricultural Show at Park Royal. The first of three intermediate halts, Castle Bar Park, which served the adjacent GWR Sports Ground, was opened on 1 May 1904, to be followed by Drayton Green on 1 March 1905. South Greenford opened much later, on 20 September 1926, in response to the building of Western Avenue (the A40) and housing and commercial development in the area.

Initially, the term 'branch' which is normally used to describe a 'dead-end' line would have been a misnomer because the local trains ran mainly between Northolt and West Ealing (Ealing Broadway from 1932) and used Greenford GWR station on the Acton to High Wycombe line. However, once the Central Line tube opened to West Ruislip on 21 November 1948, the GWR station closed. Auto trains from Old Oak Lane along the Birmingham line were withdrawn, as were Ealing Broadway services travelling beyond Greenford. The latter trains now terminated at Greenford and were diverted into a dead-end bay platform between the Eastbound and Westbound lines at the new Underground station, arguably making this now a branch line for passenger services. Through freight traffic naturally continued to use the connecting spurs between the two main lines.

The Greenford services were among the first to use the new steam railmotors built in the early 1900s. These vehicles consisted of a push-and-pull carriage incorporating a small vertically-mounted steam engine. The railmotors were ideal on easier graded routes but auto trains, involving normal locomotives fitted with apparatus to enable push-and-pull carriages to be propelled, were introduced from autumn 1904 where additional power was required. By the 1930s, the surviving railmotors were wearing out, so the steam engines were removed and the vehicles converted into normal auto trailers. Some of these worked into the 1950s on the Greenford service alongside their modern counterparts which included the two named trailers from the BR built batch, *Wren* and *Thrush*. Of the 99 GWR railmotors built, only one converted vehicle survives: No 212, formerly railmotor No 93, which resides at Didcot. An appeal has been launched by the Great Western Society to fund the ambitious and remarkable task of reconverting this unique carriage to an operational steam railmotor once more.

The Greenford branch was very familiar to me as a child, not just through my train-spotting activities at Ealing Broadway and West Ealing but because I had a schoolfriend who lived close to Castle Bar Park Halt. He was not interested in railways but was always keen to play 'cowboys and indians' in the fields and woods on the eastern side of the Greenford line. Although I already knew most of the locomotives working the push-and-pull trains – Nos 5410, 5420, 1415, 1426, 1436, 1446, 1458 (the first green one I saw) and 1474 – I always kept a notebook and pencil in my pocket in order to spot potential 'cops' working freight trains. The panoramic view from Castle Bar Park towards South Greenford gave me time to break off from the games and head towards the railway line. I was particularly anxious to spot an ROD 2-8-0 because the class was rapidly diminishing; I often imagined that one was coming towards me but invariably it turned out to be a '28xx' or '38xx' 2-8-0. But at last I was rewarded. The sense of excitement in seeing No 3031 approaching Castle Bar Park Halt remains with me today, matched only by another of my rarest 'cops' a couple of years later: a Cardiff-based 2-8-2 tank No 7202 (now preserved at Didcot) which passed through West Ealing on 31 July 1959 hauling an up parcels train. I considered this working so unusual that I submitted my one and only sighting report for publication in *Trains Illustrated*.

◄ No sign of *Wren* or *Thrush* – instead No 1426 is hauling an elderly Edwardian auto trailer and another dating from the early 1930s. This view of a Greenford-bound push-and-pull leaving Drayton Green Halt was taken just before dieselisation in August 1958. *Author's Collection*

The Greenford services continue today but my interest in them ended abruptly on 25 August 1958 when the auto trains became an early victim of dieselisation. By this time, I had developed a particular affection for the archaic-looking '14xx' (previously '48xx') 0-4-2 tanks as had four schoolboys (then unknown to me) who train-spotted from the footbridge overlooking Southall shed where the tanks were based. Like me, they were disappointed to find that no 'Fourteener' was included in BR's published list of locomotives chosen for preservation and decided to remedy this in 1961 by forming the '48xx' Preservation Society, quickly changing the name to the Great Western Preservation Society and then shortening this to the Great Western Society. The society, which is today still under the chairmanship of member No 1 and also counts No 3 as a driver and the raffle promoter (two of the four schoolboys), was successful in purchasing No 1466 and auto trailer No W231 and has since gone from strength to strength. The Greenford push-and-pull services played their part as catalyst.

A Warwickshire Railway Society special from Birmingham to Swindon Works via the Greenford loop coasts round the curve south of Castle Bar Park Halt behind No 7029 *Clun Castle* on 3 April 1965. *Author*

Newly arrived in the London area, small prairie No 5569 shunts beside the Greenford branch at West Ealing in December 1963, watched by a former City of Oxford AEC Regal bus. *Author*

Excitement came to the West Ealing-Greenford line on 2 March 1958 (as it also had on 16 February) when the renewal of the Willesden to Acton Central overbridge, east of Acton Main Line station, caused the closure of the West of England line between Old Oak Common and West Ealing. Auto trains ran from Acton to Southall and a bus service covered the Greenford branch which was carrying all the main-line trains. No 6002 *King William IV* hauls an up express through Castle Bar Park Halt. *Colin Hogg*

The 3.30pm Paddington to Penzance passes Castle Bar Park Halt behind No 4090 *Dorchester Castle*. *Colin Hogg*

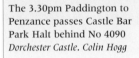

'Castle' class No 5043 *Earl of Mount Edgcumbe* hauls a Paddington-bound train over the west curve and through Drayton Green Halt under the watchful gaze of a spotter up a tree. The familiar GWR pagoda huts are a rare sight today but two fine specimens are still in use at Denham Golf Club Halt between Gerrards Cross and West Ruislip. No 5043 became another Barry scrapyard escapee and awaits restoration at the Birmingham Railway Museum, Tyseley. *Colin Hogg*

The 2.55pm Paddington to Milford Haven approaches Drayton Green Halt headed by No 5016 *Montgomery Castle*. Blocks of flats built on a tunnel have replaced the allotments. *Colin Hogg*

Small prairie No 5508 stands at Uxbridge (Vine Street) with a parcels train on 10 July 1964. The historic church and clock tower are enduring landmarks but there is no trace of the station today.
Roy Hobbs

Another Victorian station still surviving today is Langley (Bucks), whose ornate roof ironwork is just visible behind *Coney Hall's* cab. This up Worcester line express was photographed in spring 1964.
Vernon Murphy

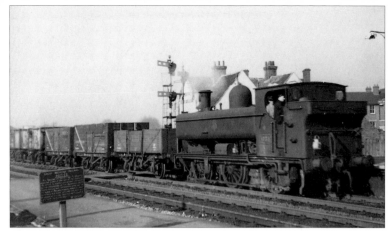

Purchased by the Great Western Society direct from Oxford shed after hauling the WR's last steam-hauled passenger train on 3 January 1966, No 6998 *Burton Agnes Hall* is seen here at West Ealing on 1 December 1962 on an up freight. *Tony Wright*

(Above right)
One of the few 'flat-cabbed' pannier tanks in the London area during the early 1960s, No 8731 hauls an eastbound freight through West Drayton on 14 February 1961. *Author*

Collett 2-8-0 No 2894 approaches Southall station with a westbound coal train. Hawk-eyed readers will also observe the Greenford auto train, an approaching express and the GWR diesel parcels railcar, No W34W. *Geoff Rixon*

7. THE BRENTFORD BRANCH

From its earliest days, the GWR had an ambition to draw freight traffic away from the rivers and canals and was particularly keen to have rail access to the River Thames near London. Brentford, where the Grand Union Canal and the River Brent run into the Thames, was close to the main line at Southall and a rail link between the two towns seemed the best option. The company therefore promoted the Great Western & Brentford Railway and Brunel was appointed civil engineer. Indeed, the line features one of his smaller masterpieces, the so-called 'Three Bridges' at Windmill Lane, adjacent to the late lamented AEC factory. The structure, carrying the road over the canal which, in turn, crossed the railway on an aqueduct, was at one time something of a tourist attraction and remains well worth visiting today since it still performs its original function.

The four-mile-long Brentford branch, which was built to the broad gauge, was opened for goods traffic on 18 July 1859 and for passenger traffic on 1 May 1860, Brentford station being located on an embankment adjacent to the High Street/London Road and ½-mile short of the Docks terminus. In 1861, a standard gauge line was added and the branch was absorbed by the GWR in 1872. Four years later, the broad gauge track was changed to standard gauge, thus creating a conventional double-track line.

The main purpose of the branch was always to carry freight. There was never much scope for attracting London-bound passengers because the LSWR provided through trains from Brentford Central station to Waterloo whereas GWR trains would have had to reverse at Southall. Nevertheless, with Western and Northern destinations in mind, the GWR made a determined effort to increase passenger traffic in the early 1900s. An intermediate stop was opened in May 1904: Trumpers Crossing (for Osterley Park) Halte. This was one of Britain's first railway halts (comprising a wooden platform and rudimentary shelter) and used the original French spelling. At the same time, the GWR introduced its new

steam railmotors and locomotive-hauled push-and-pull trains. A cross between the two, a locomotive encased to look like a short carriage to match the auto trailer, was also used on the line. There were four such conversions – two '517' class 0-4-2 tanks and two '2021' class 0-6-0 pannier tanks – but the casing was soon removed because the engines were difficult to service and were aesthetically unsuitable for other work as the size of the mock windows matched those of an auto-trailer.

Despite these efforts, passenger traffic remained sparse and services were withdrawn when World War 1 broke out. Services resumed in 1920 but insufficient use of Trumpers Crossing caused its closure on 30 January 1926 and, following the outbreak of World War 2, passenger services ceased permanently on 4 May 1942. Goods traffic continued to thrive for a time, but the line was singled in December 1955 and freight services to Brentford Dock were withdrawn on 31 December 1964. The bridges over the Great West Road and the High Street were subsequently removed but freight services continued to use Brentford Town goods yard, just north of the Great West Road, until 1970. This cessation should have sealed the line's fate but the construction of a waste transfer station on the site of the goods yard has kept the line in business to the present day.

Although I used to cross the Brentford branch twice (at the Three Bridges and at the back of the AEC factory) when I cycled from Ealing to Southall shed, I never paid much attention to the line and only rarely saw a train (always a pannier tank either hauling a goods train or travelling light engine). Standing on the footbridge between Southall station and the front of the shed, I always found it hard to pick out the Brentford line from the maze of tracks. The branch trains seemed to thread their way through the depot site, although this is perhaps not so surprising given that the original Southall shed was built in 1859 purely to serve the Brentford line. Also, the railmotor/auto-trailer shed and sidings were located on the opposite side of the branch.

When I was 13 my interest in the line increased through finding a picture of Trumpers Crossing Halte in a library book. Knowing that the halt had long since closed, a friend and I thought it would be exciting to take the book with us and try to locate the site. Leaving our bicycles at the Three Bridges, we walked along the line and were surprised how rural it was (and, remarkably, still is today). We headed towards Trumpers Way but found no traces so we turned back and examined the area near the end of Green Lane. We discovered some iron railings in the undergrowth between the track and the canal and concluded this was the correct location.

Apart from seeing a couple of steam railtours on the line in the 1960s, I have never returned, and neither has steam. The branch would seem to be ideal for an operating day with an auto train which, though mooted in the past, has never materialised. But we can always live in hope.

An unidentified 'Hall' speeds through Southall on the 10.55am Paddington to Pembroke Dock in 1957. The engine shed is in the distance, on the right. The station staff were doubtless proud of their horticultural skills. *Mike Esau*

Another unidentified engine, this time a 'Castle', hauls an up express through another well-tended station, West Drayton & Yiewsley, in 1958. The first carriage is an LNER Thompson vehicle. *Mike Esau*

Iver station opened in December 1924. The last GWR-built 'Castle', No 7007 *Great Western*, rushes through on an up express in 1958. *Mike Esau*

An immaculate Churchward Mogul, No 5332, heads an up freight near Iver (the station is seen through the bridge) on 7 May 1960. The locomotive is unusual in having retained its inside steampipes. *Colin Hogg*

8. THE UXBRIDGE BRANCH

The first GWR branch line between Paddington and Slough was the 2½-mile line from West Drayton & Yiewsley, through Cowley, to Uxbridge (Vine Street), which opened on 8 September 1856. Following the construction of the Great Western/Great Central joint line from Northolt Junction to High Wycombe, the GWR built a branch from Denham to Uxbridge (High Street) which opened on 1 May 1907. The terminus was built on a brick viaduct with the intention of joining the two GWR stations and providing a circular train service to London. A bridge was constructed across the High Street but the connecting spur never materialised and the bridge was subsequently removed in 1922, leaving the brick piers to puzzle future generations.

The reason for not proceeding with the link was very simple. In 1904 the Metropolitan Railway had reached Uxbridge and by the following year was operating electric trains direct to London. It was pointless for the GWR to compete for this traffic.

With the added benefit of an electric tram route to Shepherds Bush (trolleybuses from 1936), Uxbridge was over-provided with public transport facilities and it was the non-electrified services which suffered. The High Street branch closed to passengers on 1 August 1939 but remained open to freight until 24 February 1964. The Vine Street line fared better, with passenger services continuing until 8 September 1962 and freight services lasting until 6 July 1964. But within a year, the track was lifted and the station site developed into a car park, with the result that all signs of the branch in Uxbridge have been obliterated. The Metropolitan Line, however, still flourishes.

GWR Railcar No W31W arrives at the delightfully sylvan station at Cowley, the only intermediate stop on the West Drayton to Uxbridge branch, on 20 May 1958. Designed originally as successors to the steam railmotors, these diesels were built between 1934 and 1942 and totalled 38 in number. *Tony Wright*

9. THE STAINES WEST BRANCH

This 6¼-mile line from West Drayton & Yiewsley was built by the Staines and West Drayton Railway Company in 1885 in an attempt to draw custom away from the LSWR route serving Staines Central. The branch was always very rural, serving only one station justifying a mandatory stop, Colnbrook, and, initially, two tiny halts, Poyle for Stanwell Moor and Yeoveney. The line terminated alongside Pound Mill in Moor Lane and the promotors, being strapped for cash, avoided the cost of constructing a new station building by converting the mill owner's house.

Passenger traffic on the line was modest; two new concrete halts, Poyle Estate Halt and Colnbrook Estate Halt, were opened in 1958 and 1961 respectively to serve local industrial estates, but traffic still declined and passenger services were withdrawn on 27 March 1965. Goods traffic continued, due to the opening of an oil depot in 1961 at Staines West on the site of the former goods yard. Unfortunately, the dreaded M25 motorway subsequently severed the line; the last oil train to West Drayton ran on 16 January 1981, whereupon the oil terminal was served by a new spur from the SR line until closure on 24 June 1991. However, the top end of the line survives due to the construction of an aviation fuel depot on the site of Colnbrook station, connected to Heathrow Airport by a pipeline. Rail traffic ceased for a while but has now recommenced, offering motorists using the M25/M4 junction the spectacle of a freight train threading its way through the motorway bridge supports.

Nothing remains of Colnbrook station except the stationmaster's house on the old Bath Road but the platform awning supports from Staines West now stand outside the refreshment building at Didcot Railway Centre. Meanwhile, the station building is enjoying its third career, serving as offices.

I visited the line on 14 February 1961 thinking that it was still operated by ex-GWR diesel railcars but was disappointed to find that a BR single-car unit had taken over. My observations in the following report may be of interest:

The Staines Branch runs from West Drayton & Yiewsley to Staines West. There is one station on the way, Colnbrook, and three tiny halts, Poyle Estate Halt, Poyle Halt (for Stanwell Moor) and Yeoveney. The line is operated by a one-coach diesel car, or two coaches in the rush-hour.

I left Ealing Broadway on the 9.18am diesel (running 8min late, of course!) which was all stations to Slough. There was a connection to Uxbridge from West Drayton, but not for Staines so I had to wait till 10.13am before the diesel car, No W55021, left from Platform 5. Just out of the station, the line turns right from the main line. The Staines line then leaves the Uxbridge line, curves left and goes beneath the main line. The branch is single-track and, in summer, is very picturesque. After about two miles comes Colnbrook station where there is a large passing loop and a goods yard. There is a station on both sides and a level crossing, with a signalbox. Just a few hundred yards further down the track on the right is a halt, made of concrete with a shelter, which calls itself Poyle Estate Halt. A little further, on the left, is a ramshackle little halt called Poyle Halt for Stanwell Moor, with a tiny hut. The last intermediate halt was Yeoveny which we passed without stopping both ways. This little halt, on the left of the line, had no hut, and not even a nameboard. It had an old board saying Platform 1. As tickets could not be bought from any of these halts, the guard would come along with a notebook and hand out a printed sheet of paper to those who got on, and collected the money. After Yeoveney the line crossed the SR Windsor line, went between the supports of a viaduct which was being built across both these lines, and arrived at Staines West. This was an overgrown dilapidated dump with an old water tower,

If ever there was a halt apparently in the middle of nowhere, this is it: Yeoveney, on the West Drayton to Staines West branch. Passing this rarely used request stop is No W31W on 27 May 1956. *Colin Hogg*

Collett 0-4-2 tank No 1426 operates a push-and-pull service into Staines West station. *Geoff Rixon*

a filthy old goods shed with smashed windows and overgrown track. The station was grimy and decaying. The ticket collector was an un-uniformed lady. The train waited for about 5min, and then set off. With the driver in the cab were the guard and a female in pointed shoes! There were very few working signals on the line: there is one at the loop at Colnbrook, one under the main line, and one where the Uxbridge line joins the Staines line, just before West Drayton station. At Colnbrook station, we passed No 3750 (81C) on the loop, with quite a long goods train. I arrived back at 11 o'clock and waited for the 11.28am train to Paddington, calling at Hayes, Southall and Ealing Broadway. It arrived dead on time behind No 5012 *Berry Pomeroy Castle* (81F) with corridor coaches, which got me back to Ealing before 12 o'clock. So ended an enjoyable trip.

◀ Following closure of Staines West station, No 6134 runs round its train of tank wagons in order to shunt them into the oil depot on 30 July 1965. *Tony Wright*

◀ A pair of GWR diesel railcars, with the irrepressible No W31W leading, offload a group of heavily laden passengers at Colnbrook station in summer 1958. *Mike Esau*

10. THE WINDSOR BRANCH

The GWR was keen to attract royal patronage and intended, at the outset, to join Windsor to its railway network either by building a connecting branch or by routeing the main line through the town. Its efforts on both fronts, however, were thwarted by Eton College which owned most of the necessary land and had the ear of the Establishment and Parliament. The College authorities even tried to prevent a station being built at Slough and although trains stopped there when the line opened in 1838 it was two years before there were any station buildings. Eventually, the College's objections to a Windsor line were overruled and the 2¾-mile broad gauge branch was constructed, sited as far as possible from the college. The railway, which was officially opened on

8 October 1849, was noteworthy for its approach to Windsor using a long timber trestle viaduct, later replaced between 1861 and 1863 by the present series of brick arches.

Queen Victoria was a regular traveller on the branch and a new Royal Waiting Room was built for her Diamond Jubilee in 1897. This was the first phase of the rebuilding of the station which was completed a year after her death in 1901. Subsequent royalty have also used the branch and in 1936 and 1952, 'Castle' class loco No 4082 (the original *Windsor Castle* and the renamed *Bristol Castle*) hauled the funeral trains conveying the bodies of King George V and King George VI on their final journeys. Nos 6000 and 6028, named after the monarchs, were unable to be used because

the 'King' class is too heavy for the line, a fact that was nearly overlooked a few years ago when *King Edward I* was due to be exhibited at Windsor station and had to be substituted by *Burton Agnes Hall*.

The Windsor branch was dieselised in 1959 but steam-hauled excursions continued to use the line, bringing a variety of 'foreign' locomotives such as LNER 'Sandringhams' and LMS 'Jubilees' to Slough shed for servicing. Tender engines had to turn on the Slough triangle because they would not fit on the shed turntable.

The Windsor branch is largely unchanged today. An intermediate stop, Chalvey Road Halt, was opened in 1928 but was declared illegal by Eton College and removed two years later. The elderly stations at Slough and Windsor are still used by the branch trains although there is now only one platform at Windsor and the line has been singled. The branch is an obvious candidate for special steam auto train workings.

◀ Proving that the GWR did not always clean its locomotives No 5035 *Coity Castle* dashes through Taplow on an up express to Paddington in the early postwar years. *Ian Allan Library/R. F. Dearden*

◀◀ There are strong Great Western Society connections in this early postwar photograph at Taplow. The down 1.18pm express from Paddington to South Wales is headed by 'Castle' class No 5051 *Earl Bathurst* which spent 25 years (from 1936 to 1961) at the same shed (Landore) and has now been at Didcot depot for even longer! On the right is the goods shed which was home to No 6106 in 1966-7 and where very successful open days were held by the GWS Reading Group. *Ian Allan Library/ R. F. Dearden*

An immaculate 'Castle', No 5096 *Bridgwater Castle*, is seen between Maidenhead and Taplow on an up Bristol express. The second carriage is still in wartime brown livery. *Ian Allan Library/R. F. Dearden*

11. THE WYCOMBE AND MARLOW RAILWAYS

What ended up as a series of local services was once a through line from Maidenhead to Oxford via Princes Risborough, cutting eight miles off the Didcot route. The Wycombe Railway opened in stages from Maidenhead (Wycombe Junction) – also known as Boyne Hill – to Oxford (Kennington Junction) and was completed in October 1864, having reached High Wycombe back in August 1854. At that stage, High Wycombe was not joined to any other railway; this did not occur until 1906 when the line from Northolt Junction was completed.

The Great Marlow Railway was the name of the 2¾-mile branch from Marlow Road (now Bourne End), the junction with the Wycombe Railway, to Great Marlow (now called Marlow). The railway opened on 28 June 1873 and boasted a splendid Italianate station building at Marlow which was mercilessly destroyed in 1967. The Bourne End to High Wycombe section, with intermediate stations at Wooburn Green and Loudwater, closed in 1970, and the track was lifted, leaving a 7¼-mile branch from Maidenhead to Marlow via Furze Platt, Cookham and Bourne End which still operates today.

As a child, I always had a soft spot for the '14xx' 0-4-2 tanks and missed them when the Greenford branch was dieselised in 1958 (although Southall retained No 1474 for a few years). I was delighted, therefore, to learn in 1960 that there was still a steam push-and-pull operating in the London area, on the Marlow branch, and that it was known locally as the 'Marlow Donkey'. As a result, I made several visits to ride on the train during its remaining two years of existence.

At the start of my acquaintance with the line, pannier tanks usually handled the Maidenhead to High Wycombe locals while '61xx' 2-6-2 tanks ('Tanner Oners') hauled the through trains from Paddington. The 'Donkey' was in the hands of two Slough-based 'Fourteeners', one of which was stabled in the tiny sub-shed at Marlow. During the last two years, the locomotives in question were Nos 1421, 1445,

1453 and 1474. Diesel multiple-units took over the Wycombe services in 1961 but the 'Donkey' continued to operate from Marlow to High Wycombe and Maidenhead.

One of the features of the Marlow branch was the mixed trains, the first that I had ever seen. It was not unusual for about a dozen trucks to be rattling behind the auto trailer from Marlow to Bourne End, where they would be detached by a pannier tank.

In its final years, the 'Marlow Donkey's' fame spread outside railway circles and reached the pages of the national press. Sadly, the reports usually concerned car accidents on the various ungated level crossings but one particular story was of a more light-hearted nature and is described later in this chapter. It is also interesting that around this time, Giles of the *Daily Express* sometimes used very accurately drawn 'Fourteeners' in his cartoons to represent the archetypal BR train.

The fateful last day of steam came on Sunday 7 July 1962 and, accompanied by my mother, I went to pay my last respects. Having attended the final day of the High Wycombe/Princes Risborough/Aylesbury auto trains in the previous month when No 1440 was bedecked with bunting, I was expecting the same for the 'Marlow Donkey' and took some flags to add to the display. The omens, however, were not promising. Due to engineering works on the Wycombe line, there was a bus service in operation, but luckily only as far as Cookham. Waiting for us with a single auto trailer was No 1421, looking smart in its lined green livery, but with no decorations. Indeed, there was no evidence whatsoever that this was the last day of steam and certainly no hordes of photographers. I kept my flags well hidden (well, I gave them to my mother!). The day was a great anticlimax and I bade farewell to No 1421 at Cookham in mid-afternoon.

I later read that there were celebrations, but these took place in the evening when services were restored to Maidenhead. Liquid refreshments were served to passengers

No 1453 takes on water at Marlow on 7 June 1960. The auto trailer has been detached to enable the locomotive to carry out some shunting. *Author*

No 9424 passes through Bourne End station sandwiched between a train of trucks on 7 June 1960. *Author*

and on the final train, the 10.20pm from Maidenhead, the communication cord was pulled several times.

The London area had said farewell to its steam push-and-pull services after nearly 60 years. All trains on the Marlow and Wycombe lines were now diesel operated except freight workings which lasted to the end of WR steam on 31 December 1965. I paid my last visit to see steam three days earlier and was rewarded by the sight of a resplendent No 6106 shunting at Wooburn Green at sunset. Little did I know that I would see this locomotive again on the Wycombe line (southern section) nearly eight years later when the Great Western Society operated a special steam service to commemorate the centenary of the Marlow branch.

My experiences on my first visits to Marlow and High Wycombe can be found below and later on in this chapter:

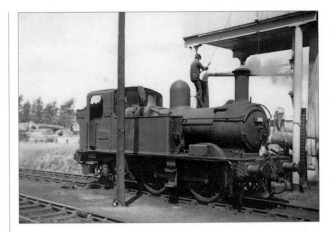

The 'Marlow Donkey' runs from Bourne End to Marlow (and sometimes from Maidenhead). To get to Bourne End, one gets a train to Maidenhead and thence on the Wycombe branch to Bourne End. On the day of my visit, the Wycombe branch engine was No 9406 with three suburban coaches. The first stop is Furze Platt Halt, then Cookham and then Bourne End. The line is a single track so a tablet is used. At Bourne End, there is a sign saying: 'Five miles speed limit, 10mph allowed for engines of the '14xx' class'. All was very quiet while we waited for the 'Donkey'. At last it arrived, from Maidenhead. The engine was No 1453 with an auto coach trailer. The engine showed signs of green paint through the dirt. It had a temporary front numberplate made of wood! The coach was in good condition, especially the interior. Well, the journey was short and sweet (single line of course)! Marlow proved to be a strange place. The engine left its coach and went to shunt. There was no signalbox, no signals, only hand-operated points which the shunter-man had to change. There was a notice board by the tiny engine shed (which houses 1453 during the night) which said: 'No 4-6-0 engines allowed in the shed'! Anyway, 1453, having shunted the trucks, went back to the coach and took us back to Bourne End, where it stayed 2min

and then returned to Marlow. Then I sat down and had my lunch. Next moment, I dived for my camera. Pannier tank No 9424 appeared from Wycombe with a truck in front of it and five behind. There was no guard's van at all. While we were waiting for the Maidenhead train, another unusual thing happened. From the Marlow line came impatient whistles. Evidently, the 'Marlow Donkey' was waiting round a curve for the signal, which was operated from Bourne End, to go down. After about 5min

◀◀ A local train to High Wycombe stands at Maidenhead hauled by No 9406 on 7 June 1960. *Author*

◀ A mixed train stands at Marlow station in summer 1961. The passengers, having walked past about a dozen trucks, are shown to the carriage. *Author*

◀◀ No 1421, on a Marlow working, takes water at Maidenhead on 31 December 1960. *Author*

◀ On the penultimate weekend before dieselisation, the driver oils the motion of No 1445 outside the tiny sub-shed at Marlow. *Author*

the impatient whistles were heard and the signal was changed. First appeared the engine, then the coach, followed by 12 clattering trucks, actually coupled on to the train! It was the first time I had ever seen a mixed train. I wouldn't have liked to have been in the coach with 12 trucks rattling behind.

Anyway, before I could see what happened to the trucks, 9406 came in with our train. So ended a very enjoyable morning.

'Marlow Donkey' Held Up By Cowboys

This and similar headlines appeared in several national newspapers on 1 December 1961. The *Daily Express* even published a night shot of the train at Marlow station, with the five personalities involved re-enacting the incident. So what actually happened?

One evening, a 'Fourteener' was propelling its single auto trailer on the 8.12pm from Bourne End when it ran over three detonators at a level crossing half a mile outside

An early morning auto train, propelled by No 1436, arrives at Windsor & Eton Central on 20 April 1958. *Trevor Owen*

No 1421 stands at Marlow station at the start of the final day of steam working, 7 July 1962, one of the most miserable days of my life. *Roy Hobbs*

A very nostalgic picture of No 1453 entering Bourne End from Maidenhead on 7 June 1960. This was my first sighting of the 'Marlow Donkey' and my very first railway colour photograph (aged 13). *Author*

Marlow station. The crew stopped the train and were alarmed to find three men emerging from the darkness dressed as cowboys. Two were masked and they all carried six-shooters. The bandits told the crew that it was a 'stick-up'. At that point, the sole passenger, who was leaning out of the window to find out what was going on, is said to have taken cover under a seat. The three men then explained that the guns were just toys and the hold-up was a stunt. They climbed into the cab and were driven into Marlow station.

The British Transport Commission was not impressed by the escapade and prosecuted the individuals. The BTC thought that the men were setting a bad example to youngsters and were also concerned about the lack of remorse shown by the culprits who regarded the matter as a huge joke. Marlow Magistrates' Court heard that on the evening in question there had been a 'certain amount of jollification' at the 90-year-old 'Railway Hotel' to celebrate its change of name to the 'Marlow Donkey'. Two of the cowboys were members of a six-piece jazz band which had

been playing in the public house and 'had certain items of fancy dress' available.

The three men, all aged 39 or 40, pleaded guilty to entering a carriage 'otherwise than on the side of a platform' contrary to railway by-laws; unlawfully and wilfully stopping 'a vehicle on the railway'; and wilfully obstructing the driver in the execution of his duty. They were fined 10s (50p) on each of the three charges and ordered to share £7 13s costs. They then returned to the 'Marlow Donkey' public house for a celebration drink. Such is the march of time that if they are still alive today, they will be approaching their eighties.

A Visit to High Wycombe

It was a bright sunny day as I set off to catch the 10.52am diesel train from Ealing Broadway to Maidenhead, with a connection to Marlow. I had already been on the Marlow line three times, but having studied the winter timetable, I discovered that on Saturdays a train left Marlow at 12 o'clock for High Wycombe, and it seemed fairly

A view of the 'Marlow Donkey' on arrival in the bay platform at Bourne End. *Author*

No 1453 has deposited a scout group at Marlow on a rare occasion when the auto trailer, this time a converted suburban coach, was the wrong way round. *Author*

obvious that this was the 'Marlow Donkey'. As I had no pictures of this section of line, I went out there to travel on this train. At 10.56am my train arrived and it was fairly crowded. We arrived at Maidenhead at 11.35am where No 1421 was waiting. This left at 11.38, and was well filled up. Two people left the train at Furze Platt and about 12 at Cookham. The rest trickled out at Bourne End, except a few, and a couple more got on, making about eight for the last 6min up to Marlow. Here we arrived at 11.59am. I then bought a single ticket to High Wycombe. At 12.4pm we left Marlow with about six passengers aboard. Having spent about 2min at Bourne End, we chuffed off to High Wycombe. The scenery on this stretch of line is slightly better than on the other section. Soon we came into Wooburn Green which, like Furze Platt Halt, has no passing loop, and therefore has a station on one side only. Now there were only four of us left in the train. After we had left Loudwater, the station before High Wycombe, we could see across the valley below an LMR 2-6-4 tank on a Marylebone local.

Soon we were joining up with the main line and we ran along it for a little way before entering High Wycombe where we arrived in bay Platform No 1. By the station I saw a '94xx' pannier tank, a '22xx' engine, and a 'Hall' on a goods. Everyone was staring at our train. I bought a ticket to Bourne End, from where I could use my Marlow-Ealing ticket, as I was going straight to Maidenhead from High Wycombe. 'The Donkey' stayed for 10min and then we were off to Maidenhead, stopping at all stations.

'The Donkey' arrived at Maidenhead at 1pm and I did not catch the 1.2pm diesel home, but the 2.2pm, giving me time to have my lunch and take some pictures of pannier tanks Nos 3608 and 9415 which came to the Wycombe line platform to take water. There was a pleasant surprise for me at 1.40pm for up came No 6143 on a five-coach train, almost full, which set off to High Wycombe.

I then caught the 2.2pm diesel home, and so ended a most enjoyable trip, with most enjoyable weather!

◀◀ My last sighting of the 'Marlow Donkey' as it terminates at Cookham during the final afternoon of steam operation. My long-suffering mother tries to avoid the camera. *Author*

◀ No 1474 stands in the bay platform at High Wycombe on one of the few Marlow to High Wycombe auto train journeys. *Author*

Three days before the
official end of WR steam on
31 December 1965 I had
another chance encounter
with the resplendent 2-6-2
tank No 6106, shunting in the
late afternoon sunshine at
Wooburn Green. *Author*

Oxford 'Tanner Oner' No 6111 trundles through Loudwater in September 1965 on a freight train, passing the Maidenhead to High Wycombe railcar in the loop. There is no sign yet of the elevated M40 motorway in this picture. *Author*

A Maidenhead train, headed by No 6131, approaches Bourne End from High Wycombe in summer 1957. *Mike Esau*

A Midlands through train to the Southern Region, hauled by No 5912 *Queen's Hall*, runs alongside High Wycombe's famous retaining wall in summer 1958. *Mike Esau*

Pannier tank No 9758 passes over Ruislip water troughs with a weedkilling train on 14 May 1960. Note the ROD tenders in the train and the spare shovel slotted in between the handrail and bunker side, lest the fireman's shovel should disappear into the firebox. *Colin Hogg*

The 3.10pm Paddington to Wolverhampton express is seen near Beaconsfield on 7 May 1960 hauled by No 6024 *King Edward I*. This lucky survivor and its Didcot-based 'son', *King Edward II* (No 6023), escaped death thanks to their excessive weight. Sold to T. W. Ward Ltd of Briton Ferry, near Neath, in October 1962, they were not allowed to travel west of Cardiff but later received special permission to be taken to Barry scrapyard, from where they were saved. *Colin Hogg*

A spotless loco, a gas-lit station, a date as late as 12 May 1965 and yet there are no admirers (except me) at Beaconsfield to appreciate No 7029 *Clun Castle* heading a VIP working of the 4.15pm from Paddington to Banbury. *Author*

A light dusting of blown snow partly covers the down platform at Seer Green & Jordans as a grimy, Old Oak Common 'Castle', No 7035, speeds through on the 4.15pm to Banbury in early 1964. The name *Ogmore Castle* was originally carried by No 5080 *Defiant*, then by No 7007 *Great Western*, before ending up on No 7035. *Vernon Murphy*

12. THE 4.15PM FROM PADDINGTON

In 1964, after the last steam-hauled express workings from London (the Worcester line trains) had been dieselised, an obscure semi-fast service was suddenly thrust into the limelight – Paddington's sole remaining rostered steam working: the Monday to Friday 4.15pm to Banbury.

When I first became acquainted with the 4.15, it consisted of a scruffy 'Hall' or 'Grange' pulling four corridor coaches (some painted green) and a General Utility Van (GUV). On one particular occasion, I remember going to Paddington and staring at the indicator board with puzzlement. There was a 4.10 express calling at Banbury and a 4.20 stopper, via Oxford, but no 4.15 to Banbury. A 4.15 to King's Sutton was shown but I ignored this at first, never having heard of that place. Eventually I spotted the intermediate stops and realised that this was the right train. The reason for Banbury not being shown was that two subsequent expresses reached there first, passing the 4.15 *en route*: Banbury-bound passengers, apart from steam enthusiasts, might catch the slow train by mistake.

Outside school holidays, my only opportunity to see the 4.15 was on Wednesdays, which was my games afternoon. Having wangled my way out of rugby and cricket and into the swimming group, my time was my own after about 3.15pm. We used the public baths at Ealing, hence the short duration of the swim, and, fortunately, the baths were virtually adjacent to the Western main line. I could therefore watch the light engine pass under Longfield Avenue bridge at about 3.30pm on its way from Southall shed to Paddington. Having recently bought a small Honda 50 motorbike but not being allowed to take it to school, I used to collect it from home at lunchtime and park it near the baths. After the light engine had passed, I had enough time to travel to the Birmingham line to photograph the train. If the locomotive was one of the surviving 'Castles' (by 1965, only Nos 5042, 7022, 7029 and 7034 remained), I would drive flat out (at 40mph) to the first stop at

Gerrards Cross and travel on the train to Beaconsfield or High Wycombe. On one occasion, when I set off early with a pillion passenger, the motorbike seized up outside Northolt Aerodrome but miraculously unseized itself after a brief cooling-off period, still getting us to Gerrards Cross in time. Three of the 'Castles' emulated the 'Halls' and 'Granges' in terms of their appalling external condition, No 7029 *Clun Castle* being the exception because it was generally kept clean for working specials. It was, in fact, the only Western locomotive I saw in the London area during 1965 which occasionally carried its brass nameplates although these, and the cabside numberplates, were normally removed for its forays on the 4.15.

As summer approached, news came that the 4.15 was to be axed at the start of the new timetable in June and I vowed to see the train as often as possible. During the final weeks, I witnessed some unusual workings on the 4.15 but before recounting these I will start with an earlier example which, although not witnessed by me, was reported in the railway press.

The date was 16 September 1964 and No D1740, which was hauling the 4.10pm from Paddington to Birkenhead, failed at Hanger Lane. Coming up behind was No 6967 *Willesley Hall* on the 4.15. The 'Hall' apparently pushed the broken-down train (it was not stated how far) while still attached to its own train, thus ending up sandwiched in a formation consisting of one dead diesel, 16 carriages and two parcels vans!

As for my own experiences, Friday 30 April was a day to remember. No 7912 *Little Linford Hall* reversed through Ealing Broadway at the normal time and I chose to photograph the train at a new location on the Birmingham line, just west of Old Oak Common. The 4.10pm diesel-hauled express passed by and I knew there were only a few more minutes to wait. I listened out for the whoosh of steam but instead heard an unfamiliar rattle growing louder. Around the curve came a four-car diesel multiple-unit displaying Banbury on the front indicator. I was horrified! Where was *Little Linford Hall*? If it had broken down, where was its train and how could it have been so promptly replaced by a multiple-unit? Disappointed, because it was a bright day, I began to head back towards my motorbike when I heard a distant steam whistle. Coming into view was a grimy 'Hall', pulling four corridor coaches and a GUV (plus four additional carriages, if I recall correctly), but it was not heading my way! Instead, it disappeared down the Western main line although I managed a distant photograph over a wire-mesh fence. An explanation subsequently appeared in the railway press. On this and the previous day, when No 6991 *Acton Burnell Hall* was involved, the trains forming the 4.15pm and 4.20pm departures from Paddington to Banbury (the latter routed via Oxford) were switched due to school parties returning to Cholsey and Radley which required additional capacity. It seems that, unknowingly, I had witnessed the last scheduled steam train out of Paddington down the Western main line, and all because, by chance, I had made my one and only visit to see the 4.15 at a point where both main lines were close by.

The next unusual event for me took place on Wednesday 12 May. I was waiting for the light engine to pass under Longfield Avenue when a resplendent *Clun Castle* in full regalia (numberplates and nameplates fitted) reversed through. However, it carried a reporting number, M48, on the smokebox which I had never seen before on the 4.15. I wondered, therefore, if the locomotive had been rostered to haul some other train. However, there was no time to wait and see if another light engine would come through. I had to take a chance and rush over to Gerrards Cross for a ride on the train. On reaching the station, I bought a ticket to Beaconsfield and was delighted when M48 came into view. When I alighted at Beaconsfield (see photo on page 90), there were no onlookers to admire the train – just one other photographer and he was riding on the footplate. I subsequently learned that the lucky fellow was Peter Lemar, Chairman of the South West Group of the Great Western Society and that the trip had been specially arranged by Chief Inspector Thorley. Accompanying Peter

on the footplate was Inspector Kerley and later in the journey he asked the crew, driver Tyler and fireman Yates, to 'have a go'. The result was a magnificent 93.5mph at Blackthorn.

The last 4.15 was due to run on Friday 11 June, but I could not be certain of getting away from school to see it. Wednesday 9 June might be my last chance but unfortunately it was a dismal day. For some reason, I missed the light engine running up to Paddington but I headed off to North Acton to photograph the train. The predictably grimy engine came into view but it was an unfamiliar shape. To my surprise the motive power was 'Black Five' No 44666, the only time I saw a non-Western locomotive in charge of the 4.15.

Friday afternoons for me involved cadet force activities which lasted until 5.15pm and nipping out of school in army uniform would be too risky. But luck was on my side – 11 June was our annual 'mufti' day when we wore normal school clothes. This reduced the risk of being spotted leaving school early. A friend was similarly minded to see the last 4.15 so we arranged unofficial cover for our duties, and crept out of school at 4 o'clock to where my trusty Honda 50 was hidden. We sped off to the nearest accessible point which commanded a good view: the footbridge in Mason's Green Lane at Park Royal. We had to cut it fine to ensure that we were back in time for final parade at 5pm.

A large crowd had turned out to see the last scheduled steam train from Paddington and, predictably, *Clun Castle* performed the honours, once more carrying the reporting number on the smokebox and, additionally, the GWR coat of arms. The extra-long train passed by quite slowly and then it was time to rush back to school. Thankfully, we had not been missed.

Photographs of the departure from Paddington appeared the following day in the national newspapers. Crowds of people had thronged the platform; even more, it seemed, than for the last broad gauge departure on 20 May 1892, not that I was there! On that occasion, a salvo of fog signals sounded; this time, a bugler played the 'Last Post'. Within a month, three of the last four 'Castles' had been withdrawn, leaving *Clun Castle* as the sole operational BR representative of this distinguished class.

Steam locomotives did turn up occasionally at Paddington during the remaining months before the official end of WR steam on 31 December 1965, but only on railtours or as substitutes for failed diesels. In early 1966, the occasional 'Black Five' appeared, providing steam-heating on diesel-hauled trains. But 11 June 1965 was the date that mattered, marking the end of an era which had begun at the first Paddington station 127 years earlier, on 4 June 1838. Of course, No 6000 *King George V* was to make a triumphant return in October 1971, but that is another story, outside the scope of this book.

In March 1965, the late afternoon sunshine just catches the 4.15pm as it leaves Gerrards Cross behind No 7925 *Westol Hall*. A wonderful array of what would now be regarded as classic vehicles, including a bubble car, fill the station car park. *Vernon Murphy*

A final view of the 4.15pm to Banbury headed by No 5933 *Kingsway Hall* passing Park Royal in May 1965, with the Guinness Brewery in the background. *Author*